REFORMING

OUR

WORSHIP

MUSIC

TODAY'S
ISSUES

# REFORMING

# OUR

# WORSHIP

# MUSIC

LEONARD R.
PAYTON

CROSSWAY BOOKS • WHEATON, ILLINOIS
A DIVISION OF GOOD NEWS PUBLISHERS

**Library of Congress Cataloging-in-Publication Data**
Payton, Leonard R., 1958–
    Reforming our worship music / Leonard R. Payton.
    p.   cm. — (Today's issues)
    Includes bibliographical references.
    ISBN 1-58134-051-6 (booklet : alk. paper)
    1. Music in churches. 2. Music in the Bible. 3. Contemporary
Christian music—History and criticism. I. Title. II. Today's issues
(Wheaton, Ill.)
ML3001.P23   2000
264'.2—dc21                           99-047563
                                                 CIP

| 15 | 14 | 13 | 12 | 11 | 10 | 09 | 08 | 07 | 06 | 05 | 04 | 03 | 02 | 01 | 00 | 99 |
|----|----|----|----|----|----|----|----|----|----|----|----|----|----|----|----|----|
| 15 | 14 | 13 | 12 | 11 | 10 | 9 | 8 | 7 | 6 | 5 | 4 | 3 | 2 | 1 | | |

# CONTENTS

# PREFACE

These are not good days for the evangelical church, and anyone who steps back from what is going on for a moment to try to evaluate our life and times will understand that.

In the last few years a number of important books have been published, all trying to understand what is happening, and they are saying much the same thing even though the authors come from fairly different backgrounds and are doing different work. One is by David F. Wells, a theology professor at Gordon-Conwell Theological Seminary in Massachusetts. It is called *No Place for Truth*. A second is by Michael Scott Horton, vice president of the Alliance of Confessing Evangelicals. His book is called *Power Religion*. The third is by the well-known pastor of Grace Community Church in California, John F. MacArthur. It is called *Ashamed of the Gospel*. Each of these authors is writing about the evangelical church, not the liberal church, and a person can get an idea of what each is saying from the titles alone.

Yet the subtitles are even more revealing. The subtitle of Wells's book reads *Or Whatever Happened to Evangelical Theology?* The subtitle of Horton's book is *The Selling Out of the Evangelical Church*. The subtitle of John MacArthur's work proclaims, *When the Church Becomes Like the World*.

When you put these together, you realize that these careful observers of the current church scene perceive that today evangelicalism is seriously off base because it has abandoned its evangelical truth-heritage. The thesis of David Wells's book is that the evangelical church is either dead or dying as a significant religious force because it has forgotten what it stands for. Instead of trying to do God's work in God's way, it is trying to build a prosperous earthly kingdom with secular tools. Thus, in spite of our apparent success we have been "living in a fool's paradise," Wells declared in an address to the National Association of Evangelicals in 1995.

John H. Armstrong, a founding member of the Alliance of Confessing Evangelicals, has edited a volume titled *The Coming Evangelical Crisis*. When he was asked not long afterwards whether he thought the crisis was still coming or is actually here, he admitted that in his judgment the crisis is already upon us.

The Alliance of Confessing Evangelicals is addressing this problem through seminars and conferences, radio programs, *modern* REFORMATION magazine, Reformation Societies, and scholarly writings. The series of booklets on today's issues is a further effort along these same lines. If you are troubled by the state of today's church and are helped by these booklets, we invite you to contact the Alliance at 1716 Spruce Street, Philadelphia, PA 19103. You can also phone us at 215-546-3696 or visit the Alliance at our website: www.AllianceNet. org. We would like to work with you under God "for a modern Reformation."

*James Montgomery Boice*
*President, Alliance of Confessing Evangelicals*
*Series Editor, Today's Issues*

# ONE

---

# The
# Music Wars

---

So what flavor would you like today? Pistachio mint or lemon fudge? Sugar cone or waffle cone? Maybe a cup instead?

Westerners demand a choice. We must have the right to choose. Truth be told, we are far more concerned that we be allowed to choose than we are about making the right choice. This is where we evangelicals have now come with our "styles" of worship. Churches even divide over this issue!

Here at the very beginning I want to say that it distresses me to risk grieving a brother or sister in Christ. But I feel strongly led to share the message of this book and to say it strongly. I urge the reader not to react to this first chapter or what follows and just put the book aside, but to keep reading, prayerfully and carefully. As Francis Schaeffer said so eloquently, we must, we simply must, come together—with tears if necessary. My intent is to clarify and heal, to call our church to its confessional roots, espoused so clearly in the Reformation. I desire to hurt no one, but I feel compelled to issue a strong call back to our true roots.

There is a disturbing trend in our midst that threatens to unravel us to the core. Pick out any five local congregations, even in the same denomination, go to their services on five successive Sundays, and you may come away with the impression that you have been to five entirely different worlds. Worship is in chaos and pandemonium, and at the center of the conflict is music.

You could go to many churches that profess to follow the Bible and find them "doing" bells and smells with vestments. Maybe the bells and smells are right, but have they arrived at this by careful theological reflection?

You could then go to many "high" churches and find "hot forties praise and worship" music. Have those churches arrived at this position by thorough theological reflection?

Others practice a kind of "American Gothic" tradition. Too frequently this tradition exults in very simple worship. Maybe they are right, but again, have they arrived at their position by meaningful theological reflection?

We are in the midst of music wars today. We have divided into factions, and these factions are not primarily theological as they used to be but frequently are due to differences over music. There are two main camps but many splinters. As we look closely, we find the labels to be misleading.

### Traditional and Contemporary Labels

Sometimes we call one camp "traditional." But when it comes to defining it, about all we can say is that "traditional" seems to be anything written before the sixties. Never mind that there is a real plethora of styles and theological perspectives from that vast time frame. The most salient feature of this kind of service is simply that it is "traditional." Both adherents and detractors of the "traditional" music seem to be satisfied with that label.

The other camp is "contemporary," meaning in many (but not all) cases whatever appeals spiritually to a white, middle-class, middle-aged, suburban American. Neil Young turned fifty a few years ago, but today a considerable faction in the church openly imitates and reveres the music of Crosby, Stills, Nash, and Young, all the while thinking it is contemporary.

This is a non sequitur. Actually, if you look at Christian Copyright and Licensing Incorporated's most recent list of the top twenty-five praise and worship choruses, you will find they are at least ten years old, and some are about twenty-five years old. The "top twenty-five" is a pretty good litmus test for what is perceived as "contemporary" within the broad, visible church, but something that is a quarter of a century old is not truly contemporary.

In November 1997 Knight-Ridder produced a syndicated article about teens and twenty-some-things going to a well-attended alternative Christian concert featuring the band Five Iron Frenzy and other groups. The article said, "These bands don't stuff their albums with old-fashioned praise and worship songs." "*Old-fashioned* praise and worship songs"! Clearly, what many churches are using for worship music is merely an alternative tradition, albeit a younger one, born of sixties, seventies, and eighties pop music.

### An Alternative Tradition

Recently a theology professor wrote a book advocating the use of contemporary worship music with an appendix listing more than 100 contemporary worship songs. The average age of the songs on that list is conservatively at least fifteen years, and more realistically it is probably closer to seventeen or eighteen years.

I was at a Piano Guild competition and had a *Twilight Zone* experience. The Piano Guild is an organization of piano teachers and school-age students that some think stodgy. A familiar melody wafted from a practice room. It sounded like a low-grade imitation Schuman. But as I listened, I realized that it was nothing other than Bob Hudson's

"Humble Thyself in the Sight of the Lord" (written in 1978; copyright 1983, Maranatha) with some ersatz classical bric-a-brac around it—a little trill here, an appoggiatura there. This song, too, can be found on the professor's list of contemporary worship songs. Does a praise and worship chorus somehow increase in validity because we bedabble it with a cambiata here and a little PDQ Bach imitative counterpoint there?

An advocate for contemporary worship music recently accused its detractors of "aesthetic snobbery." But it is not aesthetic snobbery to identify something as cheap and tawdry if it really is. As followers of the Truth, we are called to be honest.

Someone recently said, "We must recognize that contemporary worship music does have a certain freshness." But a lot of it doesn't. We might have been able to say that twenty years ago, but not now.

What we are dealing with here is not really "contemporary" but rather an *alternative tradition*. So the real question is not whether you will be traditional or not, but rather, which tradition will you embrace? The contemporary spirit is defined not so much by a style as by its demand for immediacy. This is what has happened to us in our mass-media-saturated culture. Anything that fails to give immediate satisfaction, that demands some reflection, is going to be perceived as unsympathetic to the needs of modern man.

So we have these principal factions, both claiming preeminent position. Each "side" clamors for recognition as legitimate, reminiscent of the factions in 1 Corinthians 1. The choice I personally think is the most dangerous, however, is the so-called blended service. In my mind, this is postmodern times come to the church, a compromise by juxtaposing theological and aesthetic streams that are not compatible at all. Obviously, not all

Christians see it this way, but I do, and I believe biblical principles support my stand. Worship and music are too powerful and important to be left to taste, to popularized compromise.

### Commercial Music

A great deal of the problem with much contemporary Christian music is that it is primarily commercial, which means that it is designed to please the greatest number of people without reminding them of the hard, demanding side of Christian faith and discipleship. Some lives have been wrecked by this music, and the growth I personally have seen come from it has been hothouse growth. It is luxuriant and beautiful, but it is short-lived, and it doesn't help us in hard times. The growth it seems to create is not buffered growth like a bristlecone pine in the southern Sierras searching for a crack in the granite so it can stubbornly force a root into the ground, a tree that will withstand the blistering, sunbaked heat of summer or the heavy snows of winter.

Most commercial Christian music does not foster "throw[ing] off everything that hinders and the sin that so easily entangles" or the trust that fixes its "eyes on Jesus, the author and perfecter of our faith, who for the joy set before him endured the cross, scorning its shame" (Heb. 12:1-2). It does not tell us to "take up [our] cross daily and follow" Jesus (Luke 9:23). It rarely encourages us to "deny" ourselves or to welcome the Lord's discipline "because the Lord disciplines those he loves, and he punishes everyone he accepts as a son" (Heb. 12:6). It does not tell us to "work out [our] salvation with fear and trembling" (Phil. 2:12). It does not prepare us to face the "tyrant's brandished steel" or the "lion's gory mane with the martyr's eye that pierces beyond the grave" (Reginald Heber, "The Son of God Goes Forth to War," 1827). Its text may tell us to "flee the evil desires of youth" (2 Tim. 2:22), its lyrics may tell us to fear God, but its style simply cannot. It does not remind us of wholesome but unpleasant facts such as, "the length of our days is seventy years" (Ps. 90:10). What it gives in its text, it takes back with its music.

### Light, Bouncy, Entertainment-Type Music

Some may object that they know many Scripture songs or praise and worship choruses that contain Scripture passages, perhaps even contemporary musical settings for beefy hymn texts. But even these are failures because the music is light, bouncy, entertainment-type music; the aesthetic *form* communicates fun and good times to most people rather than serious worship of Almighty God. Furthermore, the form may be heard with more lasting impact than the words, no matter how correct and noble the ideas in these songs may be.

There is a sharp cognitive dissonance here that the outsider often recognizes immediately because his life is basically a hedonistic or nihilistic party. He *knows* those forms intimately, and he knows they are inconsistent with the message of the words. Party music is inferior evangelistic music, for as Calvin Johannson says wisely, the way one comes to faith in Christ has profound implications for what that person will expect subsequently of the Christian life (*Discipling Music Ministry*, Peabody, Mass.: Hendrickson, 1992, p. 15).

There is another problem with using Christian "party" music—we are not ready for the party yet. There *will* be a party. And it will far exceed any party any of us has ever experienced. But right now we are being buffeted and refined. We are being purged and pruned and chastened. And if we are not, we are not God's children. Suffering is normal in the Christian life. Could it be that our music actually fosters chafing against

God's fatherly chastening, against the growth he so lovingly intends for us?

### American Gothic Traditional

Not nearly as much needs to be said here. Many, many of us grew up on hymns. Some of them are grand, some mediocre, and some just plain schmaltzy. It must be remembered, too, that any number of hymns now passing for traditional were the "contemporary" Christian music of *their* day. So be it. But the problem is that too often Christians engage in mindless singing, assuming it must OK because it is old, relatively speaking. You are not worshiping God if you are merely mouthing the old standby words from the hymnals in the pews.

The problem here is much the same as with contemporary Christian music. We just like this schmaltzy stuff because it reminds us of the worship music Eisenhower may have liked or what the Cleavers heard when they went to church. It is still musical appetite that rules—no more, no less here than in the contemporary tradition. Your mind and heart can be as easily disengaged here as with more recent worship music.

As I have thought again and again about these issues, I have repeatedly come up against this perplexing situation. My life would be easier if I could demonstrate that the purveyors of commercial Christian music were sprouting horns and carrying pitchforks, but I cannot. I have noticed that regardless of which camp we are in, we all seem to love the same Lord, we all seem to want to see people come to faith in Christ, and, most perplexing of all, we all believe that what we are doing musically glorifies God and edifies people and, in some cases at least, that the other person's music does not.

*This* is the crux of our worship music wars. We must see that though we take different stances on all this, we are not enemies at all. Our true enemy, the devil, is always searching for chinks in our armor, and now he has found one—our musical appetites; so he pokes at it with glee. As Allan Bloom points out in *The Closing of the American Mind* (New York: Simon & Schuster, 1987, p. 68), almost nothing matters as much now as music. This, he says, is a big change from even recent generations. With judgments, aesthetic and otherwise, being reduced to taste, it is no wonder that the devil finds us weak here. This is why we are fighting now about music but were not just a few short years ago. We haven't really changed much theologically. What has happened is that our enemy has found a chink, and now it is open season.

If I am correct in my analysis, this should be comforting news, for in identifying our flaw, we will be on the way to reformation and an end to the worship music wars.

# TWO

---

# The
# Levitical Musicians

---

The Westminster Confession of Faith says of gathered worship, "The reading of the Scriptures with godly fear, the sound preaching and conscionable hearing of the Word, in obedience unto God, with understanding, faith and reverence, singing of psalms with grace in the heart, as also the due administration and worthy receiving of the sacraments instituted by Christ, are all parts of the ordinary religious worship of God" (chapter 21, section 5). The Westminster divines supported all their statements with Scripture texts, and here they turned to Colossians 3:16, NKJV.

> *Let the word of Christ dwell in you richly in all wisdom, teaching and admonishing one another in psalms and hymns and spiritual songs, singing with grace in your hearts to the Lord.*

The Puritan approach to gathered worship is not to do anything unless it is specifically commanded in Scripture, and then we *must* do it. What this means here is that the Westminster divines believed—and I believe with them—that Colossians 3:16 is not about private piety but principally about gathered worship.

### A Musical High Point

We can see the implications of this by looking at one of the high points of biblical music history. We are told in 2 Chronicles 20 that messengers came to King Jehoshaphat one day and told him that an army of Moabites, Ammonites, and Meunites were coming against him from Edom and were already at En Gedi. En Gedi is about halfway up the west coast of the Dead Sea and only about twenty miles from Jerusalem. So this was a dangerous situation. Jehoshaphat proclaimed a fast and sought wisdom from God, asking for deliverance.

While the people were standing before the Lord with their wives and children, the Spirit of God came upon a man whose name was Jahaziel, the son of Zechariah, a Levite of the sons of Asaph. He said, "Listen, King Jehoshaphat and all who live in Judah and Jerusalem! This is what the LORD says to you: 'Do not be afraid or discouraged because of this vast army. For the battle is not yours, but God's. Tomorrow march down against them. They will be climbing up by the Pass of Ziz, and you will find them at the end of the gorge in the Desert of Jeruel. You will not have to fight this battle. Take up your positions; stand firm and see the deliverance the LORD will give you'" (2 Chron. 20:15-17).

We know from Jahaziel's heritage that he was a Levitical musician, and the significance of this will become clear later in the story.

Levitical musicians kept two-week tours of duty in Jerusalem just like the priests and the door-keepers did, and they were probably also present during the three major feasts. But what did they do the rest of the time? Here we are helped by other passages. In 1 Chronicles 6 we are told that the Levites received no tribal territory for an inheritance in Israel. Rather, they received towns and fields throughout the land. The priests had towns in Judah, Benjamin, and among the half tribe of Ephraim—that is, close to Jerusalem. But the other Levitical families were scattered around the country. Since the musicians were only in Jerusalem two weeks plus holidays each year, are we to suppose they just sat on the porch and discussed the weather the rest of the time? I think not.

First Kings 4:31 tells us that Solomon was even wiser than "Ethan the Ezrahite, Heman, Calcol and Darda, the sons of Mahol." I do not know who Calcol and Darda were, but Heman and Ethan were two of the original three chief musicians (Asaph being the other). So the Scriptures are telling us in so many words, "Take Solomon out of the picture, and two of the wisest men in all the land were musicians."

Is that how you view musicians today? When you think of the wisest men of our day, do images of musicians spring to mind, many of them wearing outlandish clothing with studs in their ears, sporting a four-day-old beard? Is your church musician the wisest person in your congregation or merely a specialist? Is your musician a teacher or an entertainer?

Wise people are supposed to teach. So we can presume that Heman, Ethan, and Asaph were Israel's teachers and that God in his providence saw to it that the best teaching was available to all his people by carefully spreading the wise men, these Levitical musicians, throughout the land. Heman was of the Levitical clan of Kohath, which had towns in the lands of Judah, Benjamin, Manasseh, and Ephraim. Asaph was of the Levitical clan of Gershom, which had towns in the lands of Issachar, Asher, Naphtali, and Manasseh. Ethan was of the Levital clan of Merari, which had towns in the lands of Reuben, Gad, and Zebulun. What they taught is embedded in the Psalms. For example, consider the midsection of Psalm 50, written by Asaph:

> *"Hear, O my people, and I will speak,*
> *O Israel, and I will testify against you:*
> *I am God, your God.*
> *I do not rebuke you for your sacrifices*
> *or your burnt offerings, which are ever*
> *     before me.*
> *I have no need of a bull from your stall*
> *or of goats from your pens,*
> *for every animal of the forest is mine,*
> *and the cattle on a thousand hills.*
> *I know every bird in the mountains,*
> *and the creatures of the field are mine.*
> *If I were hungry I would not tell you,*
> *for the world is mine, and all that is in it.*
> *Do I eat the flesh of bulls*
> *or drink the blood of goats?*
> *Sacrifice thank offerings to God,*
> *fulfill your vows to the Most High,*
> *and call upon me in the day of trouble;*
> *I will deliver you, and you will honor me."*
> (vv. 7-15)

That is substantive teaching. Then the psalm turns to those who have been doing evil things:

> *". . . you thought I was altogether like you.*
> *But I will rebuke you*
> *and accuse you to your face.*
> *Consider this, you who forget God,*
> *or I will tear you to pieces, with none to rescue:*
> *He who sacrifices thank offerings honors me,*
> *and he prepares the way*
> *so that I may show him the salvation of God."*
> (vv. 21-23)

Strong doctrine from one of the wisest of Israel's Levitical teachers!

Or consider these words by Heman from Psalm 88:

> *You have taken my companions and*
> *loved ones from me;*
> *the darkness is my closest friend.*
> *(v. 18)*

That is the last verse of the psalm, which is, hands down, the bleakest of all the psalms—not very joyous, not very worshipful by our standards. But isn't it possible that these are wise words and that there is something wrong with our standards?

Psalm 89 was composed by Ethan the Ezrahite. It is fifty-two verses long, and it roams over all sorts of didactic territory. This is no trite worship chorus!

These psalms are doctrinally dense. In contrast, many today do not believe our music is to have a significant teaching function. These psalms are not in the Bible just to make us feel good about being gathered in worship. They are not emotional meat tenderizer before the sermon. They are powerful teaching vehicles, and their example demands that we approach our singing in this way too.

### A Typical Levitical Musician

Suppose you are a Levitical musician living in the land of Zebulun and that you play the psaltery. It's the middle of the day and hot. You fed your chickens and your sheep early, and now you are sitting under your fig tree practicing your instrument. In fact, you are teaching your children to play the psalter, for the day is coming when they will need to replace you in your responsibilities.

Your Zebulunite neighbor comes down the road on his way to a nearby town to visit his cousin. You hail him: "Brother Zebulunite, come sit in the shade and learn the songs of Zion for a bit."

He rests and rejoices. As a happy Levitical

musician, you catechize him in the liturgy so your fellow Zebulunite can better understand and participate when the cantor in Jerusalem sings, "Now may all Israel say . . ." After a while the Zebulunite returns to the road, thanking his Levite brother heartily, and as he starts out he murmurs to himself, "I love the Feast of Tabernacles. 'I rejoiced with those who said to me, "Let us go to the house of the LORD"'" (Psalm 122:1).

This is a bit fanciful, of course. Perhaps the Levitical musicians catechized in other formal ways as well. I think that is likely. Whatever the case, we know that over the centuries the Levites were quite successful in their endeavors, for Matthew and Mark report rather matter-of-factly that after the Last Supper, Jesus and his disciples sang a hymn and then went out to the Mount of Olives. This hymn was nothing other than the Egyptian Hallel (Psalms 113—118), a block of Holy Scripture sung during and concluding the Passover Meal, sung *from memory by every household*.

There was no "turn in your hymnal to number 283." It was *a memorized tradition*, the same one that belonged to those who were present on the Day of Pentecost. Those people knew the Scriptures. They knew them deeply, so that when Peter applied them, the Holy Spirit worked within that large crowd. I maintain that real church growth simply cannot happen without the word of Christ dwelling richly in the congregation, without a deep, commonly held, memorized tradition, a common language of faith that has a clear and precise depth of meaning.

### The Rest of the Story

Jehoshaphat and the people got up the next day and went out as the Lord had commanded through Jahaziel. As they entered the Desert of Tekoa, Jehoshaphat brought the company to a halt. Tekoa is about nine miles south of Jerusalem, and the Pass of Ziz is maybe three or four miles to the east of Tekoa. We can assume that they had already walked a few miles and that they had a few more miles to go. There Jehoshaphat exhorted the people, "Have faith in the LORD your God and you will be upheld; have faith in his prophets and you will be successful" (2 Chron. 20:20). Anxiety must have been mounting as the people approached the pass where the enemy lay in wait. Jehoshaphat took this action to calm them. What he did showed how wise and godly he was.

Now we come to perhaps the most peculiar part of the story. Jehoshaphat then appointed singers who led the people in praising God "for the splendor of his holiness" (v. 21) as they went out before the army. They were to say:

> "Give thanks to the LORD,
> for his love endures forever." (v. 21)

The first thing we might think when we read these words is that they sang about the beauty of God's holiness as a kind of praise chorus. Like this:

> Praise the Lord!
> Praise the Lord in the beauty of holiness!
> (repeat)
> Beautiful and holy is the Lord, is the Lord.
> Beautiful and holy is the Lord.
> Holy is the Lord.

With our habits of praise and worship choruses, we can easily imagine the people singing this song as well as other praise and worship choruses based on the text "Give thanks to the LORD, for his love endures forever." But once they had done that, they would still probably have had several more miles to go, and Jeshoshophat was trying to help them pass the anxious miles in a way that would prepare them to meet the enemy.

The other modern way we might treat this story is to assume that what Jehoshaphat and the others did was to stop and listen to a sermon on why we should praise God in the beauty of holiness and about our Christian duty to be thankful to God for his everlasting mercy. Because the occasion was so important, the sermon would probably run five or ten minutes longer than planned, closing with an abbreviated hymn.

We can be sure that this all-too-common modern pattern was *not* what they relied on that day in the wilderness. Jehoshaphat's instructions to the Levites were probably a kind of musical shorthand, something like, "Here is the type of psalm to sing on this occasion." Indeed, we find these exact words in several psalms and variants of them in others.

For example, in 1 Chronicles 16 we read:

> *Ascribe to the LORD, O families of nations,*
> *ascribe to the LORD glory and strength,*
> *ascribe to the LORD the glory due his name.*
> *Bring an offering and come before him;*
> *worship the LORD in the splendor*
>     *of his holiness.*
> *Tremble before him, all the earth!*
> *The world is firmly established;*
>     *it cannot be moved.*
> *Let the heavens rejoice, let the earth be glad;*
> *let them say among the nations,*
>     *"The LORD reigns!"*
> *Let the sea resound, and all that is in it;*
> *let the fields be jubilant, and everything*
>     *in them!*
> *Then the trees of the forest will sing,*
> *they will sing for joy before the LORD,*
> *for he comes to judge the earth.*
> *Give thanks to the LORD, for he is good;*
> *his love endures forever. (vv. 28-34)*

This is the midsection of the psalm David had handed to the musicians when they brought the Ark of the Covenant into Jerusalem. That had been a glorious day, and the memory of it would have been encouraging to Jehoshaphat's people as they went forward.

Psalm 29 also contains some of these cited words.

Psalms 106 and 107 each begin with the words, "Give thanks to the LORD, for he is good; his love endures forever."

Psalm 118 is bookended by this same admonition.

Psalm 136 repeats the words "for his love endures forever" twenty-six times, responding to a recital of the many mighty acts of God in Israel's history.

Scholars are divided regarding the dates of authorship of these psalms. So we have no certainty that these exact psalms were sung on this particular occasion. Parts of the psalms are probably older than others, and successive generations probably built on the work of previous ones. But we do know that the period from David's day until a century or two after the Babylonian exile was a compositionally fertile time. Solomon alone wrote 1,005 psalms! People who experience redemption have much to write and sing about! God's people have always enumerated and exalted his redemptive actions in song. For the redeemed, praising God is like eating, sleeping, and breathing. The best songs, those inspired by the Holy Spirit and recognized by the people of God as speaking with the voice and authority of God, were brought together and became the 150 biblical songs in our Psalter.

Some psalms, such as 124 and 129, have explicit musical instructions for the congregation's participation. Others may have had heavy congregational participation, and the evidence that leads us to suspect this is the amount of deliberate repetition, like Psalm 136 that repeats the words "his love endures forever" again and again.

Some people blast praise and worship choruses for their repetitiveness. But with psalms like this in hand, that objection will not fly. Repetition is not evil in and of itself. In fact, it is often quite good. The problem is not whether or not to repeat something, but rather what to repeat and how to repeat it. The problem is *mindless* repetition, or repetition of the soft and fuzzy parts we like to the exclusion of full-orbed teaching.

So there were Jehoshaphat and his people, marching down the road to meet an enemy of superior force, singing these songs, eating up the miles. As they sang, the Lord set an ambush for the enemy. The Ammonites and Moabites turned on the men from Mount Seir, destroying them; and when they had done that, they turned on each other until not a man was left standing. All the while God's people were praising him in the beauty of his holiness and for his everlasting mercy. When they came to a watchtower that looked out over the wilderness, they saw dead bodies everywhere. It took three whole days to collect the spoil.

### The Nature of Biblical Praise Music

What have we learned about the musical tradition of Israel from our study of Jehoshaphat and the way his armies approached battle at the Pass of Ziz? Here are three systematic observations about what it means to have the word of Christ dwelling in us richly, based on our study. Our songs must be:

1. *Doctrinally dense.* Martin Luther said that the psalms are the entire Bible in miniature, but in the most beautiful form.

2. *Presented in aesthetic, not discursive, forms.* The psalms are not sermons. Aesthetics is the field of thought that concerns itself with beauty of form.

3. *Communally memorized.* Most Protestants chafe at fixed forms, but Jehoshaphat's people had flexibility precisely because they already had their fixed forms in place. It is almost a truism that those who commit entirely to extemporaneity are those who are in the deepest, most habitual ruts.

We truly have worship music wars today. The "traditional" camp gives at least lip service to doctrinally dense aesthetic forms. But by and large theirs is not a memorized tradition. It is not communally owned, which is one reason it has hit rocks and shoals in our time. On the other side, there is the "contemporary" service with its praise and worship choruses. To its credit it understands that communally memorized forms are important. But we are kidding ourselves if we think it is doctrinally dense. On the whole, the word of Christ does not dwell in us richly. But it should, and it must if we are to have a true reformation.

# THREE

---

# From the Reformation Until Now

To understand the kind of anarchy we are currently experiencing in worship music and why we have it, we need to go a long way back—to the Arian heresy and the effects it had on the church in the fourth, fifth, and sixth centuries.

Arius reasoned that since Jesus is the Son, he must have come from the Father and was therefore a created being. He was not really God. As this position emerged, the theologians of the church got together, and in A.D. 325 they decreed that Arius was a heretic. They burned his writings, banished him to what we recently knew as Yugoslavia, and were confident they had defended the peace and purity of the church. It was a misguided confidence. Arius and his followers fought back by inventing easy, likable songs—praise and worship choruses if you will—that conveyed their heresy. With these songs the heresy spread around the perimeter of the empire like wildfire and then began to move in on Rome like a tightening tourniquet.

The situation became so desperate that the theologians met again in A.D. 367, at the Council of Laodicea, and banned all congregational singing. You can guess what happened. If we banned congregational singing today, people would still listen to their contemporary tapes. A similar phenomemon occurred then.

In fact, the tide didn't really begin to turn until the theologians realized they had to take proactive control of the music, whereupon the church entered one of the golden ages of orthodox hymn writing. One of the earliest and best known examples is Prudentius' hymn "Of the Father's Love Begotten," written in A.D. 405. The *Gloria Patri* is embedded in the last verse:

> *Christ, to thee, with God the Father,*
> *And, O Holy Ghost, to thee,*
> *Hymn and chant and high thanksgiving,*
> *And unwearied praises be;*
> *Honor, glory and dominion,*
> *And eternal victory, evermore and evermore.*

When the theologians of the fifth century reflected on what had happened, they formulated the famous Latin phrase, *lex orandi, lex credendi.* Roughly translated, that means, "as one worships/prays/sings, that's how one will believe."

What is so stunning here is that the theologians of the Nicene Creed had begun the fourth century with the assumption that the content would control the form, but going into the fifth century they realized that forms control the content every bit as much. In other words, systematic theology is necessary, but it will be less than fully effective if the worship forms do not enforce the theology. For the untutored populace, the form must precede the content as a first step toward maturity, for form is the first thing one encounters. It is like a child learning to speak. Any attempt to deal with content without simultaneously dealing with the form is futile. One significant reason the Arian heresy made such inroads was because the church had no biblically comprehensive treatment of music at the time.

### A Look at Church History

If you name the name of Christ, by and large your lineage can be traced back to one of four major branches of the church. The trunk is the early church, which divided into two main branches around A.D. 1000—the Eastern Orthodox and the western church, which eventually became the Roman Catholic Church. Then the Roman Catholic Church divided in the mid-sixteenth century into Roman and Protestant branches. When the Protestant branch split off, it immediately broke into Lutheran and Reformed branches.

If you are not Eastern Orthodox, Roman Catholic, or Lutheran, your twig connects back to the Reformed church. If you are Presbyterian, Baptist, Methodist, Bible church, Disciples of Christ, Episcopalian, the Vineyard, Plymouth Brethren, Assemblies of God, Foursquare Gospel, Nazarene, Church of God in Christ, Christian and Missionary Alliance, and almost all nondenominational churches, you are an heir of the Reformed tradition. Your understanding of worship music has its context in Reformed thinking. Many of our present problems can be traced to developments within the Reformation.

When Luther began the Reformation, literacy in Germany was as low as 3 percent by some estimates. Since the church was in a dismal state, Luther grabbed for any means he could find to implement reformation. He fostered the development of schools. He translated the Bible into vernacular German. He established worship services in the language of the people instead of Latin. He wrote copious tracts.

One effort especially consumed Luther's attention, the writing of the *Small Catechism*, which he completed in 1528. When Luther was an old man, a man named Wolfgang Capito asked him which of his many writings he valued most, and he responded that only *The Bondage of the Will* and the *Small Catechism* were worth keeping.

The *Small Catechism* divides into six parts, and the heading of each part states that it is presented "as the head of the family should teach it in a simple way to his household." Those parts are: 1) the Law, expounding the Ten Commandments; 2) the Gospel, explaining the Apostles' Creed; 3) the Lord's Prayer; 4) Baptism; 5) Confession, Absolution, and the Office of the Keys; and 6) the Lord's Supper.

Luther was a competent musician. So he composed hymns, both text and melody, to flesh out each of those components. There were Roman Catholic church leaders in the middle of the sixteenth century who believed they would have been able to suppress "that Lutheran Heresy," as they called it, except for its hymnody. Samuel Taylor Coleridge maintained that as well. Whether this is extravagant or not, Luther really did understand that singing in gathered worship will directly affect what one believes. "*Lex orandi, lex crendendi.*" So we can see why Luther would say, "We shouldn't ordain young men to the ministry unless they be well exercised in music." Or again, "The theologian who knows nothing about music is worthless to me."

Luther loved and promoted music. He spoke of it as a blessing surpassed only by theology. He was aesthetically discerning, and he held a robust and vigorous view of music. He was the true impetus behind a profound church music culture that grew for several centuries, culminating in the church music of J. S. Bach, arguably the best composer ever.

In the 200 years following Luther, the Lutherans wrote about 100,000 hymns, many of which are in our hymnals today. If you look in a secular anthology of German poetry, you will find that Lutheran ministers and their hymn writing dominated the field throughout the seventeenth century, with the sole exception of courtly writing, which had nothing to do with religion.

### Two Fatal Blows

But Lutheranism was to suffer a debilitating blow from late-seventeenth-century Pietism. Pietism laid stress on personal Bible study, which is good, but also on personal experience, which invites feeling and subjectivity as measuring tools, a bad turn. Composers quickly got the message, however: "The quality of our work will be judged solely and directly by the degree of religious fervor it produces in other people. So, composers, don't play esoteric art games; park your brains at the door." This affected everyone. Consequently, the church has not produced a great composer since the death of Bach in 1750. As the great musicologist Charles Sanford Terry put it: "Bach was the last prophet of the tradition, as old as European civilization itself, that music was the handmaid of religion."

It was inevitable that Pietism, with its emphasis on subjective experience, would corrode the strength of the external, liturgical forms that previously shaped one's piety. Those forms were the moorings of Lutheranism, and Lutheranism subsequently suffered heavy blows from the Enlightenment. Pietism failed to cultivate the ground of external, objective truth. Enlightenment scientism found that house swept clean but empty and took up residence. From that day to this, Lutheranism has lived but as a surviving remnant, not a true cultural force.

On the Reformed side was Ulrich Zwingli, the Swiss reformer who was contemporary with Luther. Like Luther, Zwingli was an accomplished musician. But unlike Luther, he was more interested in the particulars of church reformation than in the central point—justification by grace alone through faith alone in Christ alone. As he surveyed the landscape of church abuses, music came in for special criticism. He claimed that to pray in one's closet (Matt. 6:6) meant to pray *silently*—that is, in a purely cerebral manner. He reasoned further that congregational singing is a type of perverted prayer. Therefore congregational singing should be suppressed.

Zwingli was not so biblically motivated as might appear on first blush, however. Church music in Zurich, where Zwingli was "peoples' priest," was a fiasco, a show put on by priests in obscure Latin. Zwingli's action was more like the desperate pragmatism of the Council of Laodicea in A.D. 367.

Of course, in Matthew 6:6 Jesus was saying nothing of that kind about prayer. He was only telling us to pray with no concern for how others might view us. Beyond that, Jesus said, "This is how you should pray: '*Our* Father in heaven . . .'" (Matt. 6:9). If Zwingli is correct, we are presented with the bizarre spectacle of hiding in our closets alone while pretending that we are somehow plural.

Once Zwingli had embraced his clumsy understanding of Matthew 6:6, he was compelled to force the rest of what the Bible said regarding gathered worship through the same press, with bad results. Thus, he says of Colossians 3:16, "Here Paul does not teach us mumbling and murmuring in the churches, but shows us the true song that is pleasing to God, that we sing the praise and glory of God not with our voices, like the Jewish singers, but with our hearts."

Colossians 3:16 does say that we are to sing with grace in our hearts. But does it then follow that such singing is a matter of silent imagination, as Zwingli would have us believe, a mere sentiment not connected with the physical, real world? Let's call this what it is, a kind of gnosticism. Worship under Zwingli was to become an ethereal, non-physical event stripped of corporeal participation as much as possible, centered entirely around the sermon. This was the earliest salvo in the history of the Reformed church regarding worship music. Thankfully, it is not the last word, but it was an inauspicious start.

### Calvin's Contribution

John Calvin came along half a generation later. He was not a competent musician; he was a lawyer. But he did realize how important congregational singing is since he regarded it as a necessity for good church order. When he was temporarily exiled from Geneva to Strasbourg in 1538, he benefited from the tutelage of Martin Bucer who had promoted a vigorous practice of congregational singing. Concurrently, Clement Marot was reducing some of the psalms to metrical poems, and people liked them and sang them to some of the commonly known folk songs and dance tunes. The idea seemed like a good one to Calvin. So he encouraged it. Calvin's musical incompetence limited his outlook and practice.

John Knox viewed Calvin's Geneva as the New Jerusalem. So the Calvinist side of congregational singing became set in stone with nowhere to develop. It would be metrical psalms only, set to dance tunes, until a precocious Isaac Watts noted about 1690 that the psalms are not overtly Christ-centered.

Calvin, like Zwingli, regarded congregational singing as prayer, thereby missing the point that it shares in the ministry of the Word by our "*teach*[ing] and admonish[ing] one another with psalms, hymns and spiritual songs."

One can account for Calvin's failure from any

of three angles. 1) The fact that people were singing psalms, hymns, and spiritual songs meant that they were also praying. 2) Calvin was so zealous to restore preaching to its position of strength that he could not conceive of the ministry of the Word occurring through a myriad of means; in this his zeal for preaching may have blinded him. 3) Calvin had probably never been exposed to a first-rate example of people teaching and admonishing one another with "psalms, hymns and spiritual songs," and because he wasn't a composer, he couldn't imagine the means to accomplish that.

We often hear that Luther began the Reformation and Calvin perfected it. Or sometimes we hear that Luther was a moderate reformer while Calvin was a thorough reformer. Yet in this most significant facet of the church's work, Luther was the thorough reformer while Calvin was underdeveloped. Luther enabled the people to teach and admonish one another with psalms, hymns, and spiritual songs, though it must be said to Calvin's credit that he also saw that the singing of psalms was essential to gathered worship.

### Heinrich Bullinger

Zwingli eradicated congregational singing altogether, but his successor, Heinrich Bullinger, who wrote the *Second Helvetic Confession* in 1562, found Zwingli's position extreme. He maintained that churches may sing. But churches that cannot sing should not be troubled by that so long as they have decent prayers and a good sermon. This overlooked God's command to let his word dwell in us richly with psalms, hymns, and spiritual songs.

The subtext here is the mistaken view that a local church is just fine as long as there is faithful preaching and praying and, further, that congregational singing is a matter of pure expediency. This is why under the banner of "Reformed" today we sometimes find consumers of the Top 40's and, on the other side, hard-bitten American-Gothic hymnody with artlessly rhymed psalms. They are both operating from the same Bullingerian philosophy of church music—namely, *everyone may do what is right in his own eyes because music does not really matter substantially or doctrinally.* Preaching is what really matters! This is the commonly shared weakness that catapulted us into the worship music wars.

Calvin circumscribed congregational music so narrowly that it could experience no sustainable aesthetic growth. Bullinger gave congregational singing the status of last week's classified ads. Is it any wonder that the Reformed church has had a patchy record at best of producing great church music composers? Reformed music was a stillborn child.

### Composers in Reformed Lands

What about the Tudor composers, men like Tallis, Farrant, Byrd, and Gibbons? What about Sweelinck? Or Handel?

As far as Tudor composers go, Thomas Tallis was a fine composer before the English Reformation began, and William Byrd remained a Roman Catholic his whole life. Thus, the lineage of Tudor music shouldn't be traced to the Reformed faith. Furthermore, the time of the later Crom-wellian Commonwealth, when Presbyterians were riding the crest of the wave, is a black hole musically, but not because music historians are out to get the Puritans. It is because there just is nothing significant to report.

Handel? Handel was not a church musician. He was a businessman whose glorious oratorios were commercial ventures that probably say more about English society of the time and its entertainment values than they do about the faith and piety of Handel.

Jan Peterzoon Sweelinck, who lived from 1562-1621, may have been the finest musician the continental Reformed church produced. He was the organist at the Old Church in Amsterdam for forty-four years. But what is curious here is that the organ was never used for gathered worship because Calvin regarded the use of musical instruments as an expression of the immature temple worship of the Old Testament Jews. The organ was used for concerts during the week. And Sweelinck was no church official in any sense. He was an entertainer. He did set the entire Genevan Psalter to choral parts, but the words were in French. This was because those settings were intended for weekday diversion only, not for gathered worship.

### Music or Preaching?

From the death of Bach in 1750 to this day, the Protestant church has not had leadership in musical culture. We have been floundering aimlessly for ten generations. The Reformed Church in her early history did a great job of sweeping out one great vile demon. But that demon has returned to an empty house, bringing seven others even more vile with him. Today we are merely trying to catch up to the world. Seeker-sensitive services are but the most extravagant manifestation of this worldly trend. Their work is not a departure of substance—contrary to what many of our polemics would indicate—as much as it is a departure of degree.

But what about the preached Word? Am I saying that singing is equal to or perhaps even above preaching? No. That would be comparing apples and oranges.

Rather, listen to what Luther, that great believer in the power of preaching, said in his treatise on the German Mass: "Since the preaching and teaching of God's Word is the most important part of divine service . . ." That sounds right, of course.

It is what we would expect Luther to say. But read the paragraph that immediately precedes that striking dependent clause, where he calls catechising children, together with the wise use of music, "child's play":

> Let no one think himself too wise for such child's play. Christ, to train men, had to become man himself. If we wish to train children, we must become children with them. Would to God such child's play were widely practiced. In a short time we would have a wealth of Christian people whose souls would be so enriched in Scripture and in the knowledge of God that of their own accord they would add more pockets, just as in the *Loci Communes* [a dogmatic work by Melanchthon that Luther admired greatly], and comprehend all Scripture in them. Otherwise, people can go to church daily and come away the same as they went. For they think they need only listen at the time, without any thought of learning or remembering anything. Many a man listens to sermons for three or four years and does not retain enough to give a single answer concerning his faith—as I experience daily. Enough has been written in books, yes; but it has not been driven home to the hearts.

That is rare candor for a preacher, but he meant it. So Luther busied himself with catechism, and that work included the vigorous preparation and teaching of a doctrinally dense hymn repertoire. By example, he was saying that if the word of Christ does not dwell richly in us, even the richest and most eloquent preaching will miss the mark.

# FOUR

# A Modern Reformation: Eight First Steps

One of the great dangers in church reformation is to identify things that need reforming, construct steps toward reformation, and then apply them directly and vigorously in a hurried, inappropriate way. Some of the Reformers suffered this defect, and "we can do," "I want it now" Americans are especially prone to this disease. But until we really believe Jesus' words when he said, "Apart from me you can do nothing" (John 15:5), there will be no serious, lasting reformation.

Had I been in Zwingli's circumstances, I would probably have abolished congregational singing.

Had I been in Calvin's position with his Ciceronian legal training, I would have heard the Renaissance sirens and been overly romantic about the apostolic church. I would probably have published a repertoire of psalms in greeting-card poetic forms and prohibited any instrumental accompaniment.

Had I been in the Puritans' shoes, I would have chafed at any fixed aesthetic forms, associating them with the injurious forms of the Church of England.

Had I been in George Whitefield's shoes, I would have left the walls of the church and hit the sawdust road, thereby inaugurating the parachurch and all the musical deviance that comes with it, for as we see today, much of the music used in the church is not made in the church, and most is controlled by business entities outside the church. I would have embraced ministry as a franchise, removing it from the direct accountability of the church. I might even have employed the bizarre techniques of Charles Finney. I would have done all those things, and so would you.

Our fathers sinned, and so have we. We too "have strayed from God's ways like lost sheep. We have followed too much the devices and desires of our own hearts. We have offended against God's holy laws. We have left undone those things which we ought to have done; we have done those things which we ought not to have done; and there is no health in us" (*Book of Common Prayer*). The word of Christ does not dwell in us richly. We need to mourn for our sins, for that is the only place a reformation of worship music for our times can start.

Still, we have to ask what specific actions we can take, and I want to end with some suggestions. These are my own faltering conjectures. I do not have as much confidence in the prescription as I do in the diagnosis. It should, however, be abundantly clear by now that I do not think there is any one model extant in current, visible American Christianity that serves the command to let the word of Christ dwell in us richly, though I suspect that the "traditional" (whatever that means) may be the best jumping-off point.

1. *We need to move away from the Renaissance, humanistic ideal of dance-form-based music toward rhythms determined by the rhythm of the text.* There are several ways of approaching this, but it will take a collective increase in compositional skill and a communal resolve to make music in new ways. The poetry in Psalms was not driven by rhyme schemes or by dance patterns. But it does have rhythm, and it treats the combination of words and ideas aes-

thetically. For that reason the poetry of the psalms comes across well in our translations. The pacing of ideas is flexible, sometimes compressed and at other times languorously elongated; and it is this very pacing that is so violated by the habit of metrical psalms. In affirming the inerrancy of the Holy Scriptures we should include the very pacing of the poetry. The form is not immaterial. The psalms do not consist of systematic treatises where the meaning is communicated by the two-dimensional values of mere words, such as one finds in legal documents or chemistry books.

2. *We should make sure that those being prepared for the ministry are also trained in music and are taught how it can be used in the best possible way in congregational worship.* I feel sorry for young pastors in our day, for nothing causes them more grief than what to do with congregational singing. These men have grown up in an age in which nearly everything that was pure, lovely, or of good report has been systematically and barbarously dismantled. They stand today on a heap of rubble with no conception of what good musical culture looks like, and yet they are to oversee the word of Christ dwelling richly in the small flocks that the Lord has entrusted to them. It is a Herculean task. They need help. They need training.

3. *We need to train our children.* Calvin provided a fine model for this in the Geneva Academy, but his goal was only to prepare preachers. We need to retool that model so we see every boy in the congregation as a potential pastor and/or church musician.

I find our sociology with its ideas of child development suspect. We usually think, "Do simple, popular, cultural things with children." But children are not predisposed to like juvenile and vapid things. A writer recently compared Prudentius' "Of the Father's Love Begotten" with

Graham Kendrick's "Shine, Jesus, Shine," a song I feel is objectionable because the music does not communicate what the words do. He said of the Prudentius text, "The hymn states too many deep doctrines too fast to be truly edifying." Earlier in the book he said that "the whole point of contemporary worship music is that it is *immediately* accessible." This man has uncritically embraced a modern American value system, not the biblical one we see in the example of Jehoshaphat and the Levitical musicians.

A reviewer came along who gave the book a warm approval. But the irony is that the reviewer is an administrator of a Christian school where the children sing "Of the Father's Love Begotten" with great gusto, and the music teacher would never teach them "Shine, Jesus, Shine."

If children *can* learn and *like* to learn difficult and veiled things, which they can, what we are really dealing with here is a matter of the will. And hasn't that been the problem with us baby boomers from the beginning? We want what we want, and we want it *now*. If we can't get it on those terms, the object must be bad; if we can get it on those terms, then the object must be good. This is a matter calling for repentance and revival, and we baby boomers need to do that in a big way. We seem to want to see how close we can get to evil with our ersatz "Christian" world-and-life-view. But we should know that when the Lord returns as Judge, nothing is going to go up in smoke faster than late-twentieth-century American pop culture. Why are we so zealous to befoul ourselves with it?

There are many bad older hymns too, of course, though worldliness has not been a prime motivating factor in the development of that music over the centuries. Still, I am prepared to concede that some of our lust for popular culture in the church has been caused by a vacuum of a well-planned and well-executed hymn practice. We can take action here immediately.

4. *Invest thought, time, and money in congregational accompaniment.* If Aunt Maude at the piano is all the church has, the pastor should call her up on Wednesday with the hymns, then go over and sing them with her once through. If you can get Aunt Maude singing, her piano will sing, and so will the congregation. We should spend money on the further education of our accompanists and upgrade the instruments in their homes so they will be more inclined to do more passionate practice.

If musicians are to make profound, theologically informed decisions for the well-being of the congregation, they need lots of study time just to figure out the why level. If we respond only to the outward demands of church music, the musician will not always appear productive. But when the Bible commands us to edify one another in psalms, hymns, and spiritual songs, the intent is to place us together in right relationships to God and one another and to transform our deep belief structures so our ethical behavior will be godly. This involves the painstaking development of wisdom. It requires reflection.

5. *Eliminate "special music" as a liturgical category.* Determine that only efficacious singing will be heard in the regular assembly. If it isn't efficacious, don't do it. The sung Word is the Word. It must meet standards of edification and intelligibility the same way the spoken Word must. Print the entire text of that which is sung in the order of worship. All Bach's cantatas were handled in this way in his day. There is certainly room for musical specialists. There are biblical examples for it. But there is no obligation to have special music between the offering and the sermon. Use musical specialists only as far as they help your other liturgical needs.

If there is a solo or choir piece in your service

that is efficacious, use it. And let the pastors pay rapt attention. God is teaching them. If the music is not truly efficacious, if it is *principally* entertaining, if it is *principally* mood-producing, then pastors should exercise their pastoral authority and get rid of it. It does not belong there.

Choirs can sing things that are efficacious that the whole congregation cannot. But that said, choirs sometimes, perhaps often, sing pieces that are theologically amorphous, poetically ghastly, and musically vacuous and conclude with a high note for the sopranos.

Choir music publishers flood the market every year with about 3,000 new pieces, and each publisher is interested in selling the greatest number of copies to the greatest number of churches. Suppose you are a music publisher, and you are considering two pieces for possible publication. One says, "Praise the Lord! Praise the Lord! [clap, clap, clap]. Praise the Lord, all the nations and be glad! Halleluia!" The other piece says, "The Lord is near to those who have a broken heart and saves those with a contrite spirit." Which one do you think you can sell more of? Clap, clap, clap, of course! We need to get real poetic and compositional skills back inside the church and out of the hands of business.

We should take the same stance toward our choir repertoires that we do toward our hymn repertoires. Throw those things away that are generic and pass time but do not really edify.

6. *Get the peddlers out of the church.* The church is responsible for the ministry of the Word, not some entrepreneurs in Nashville or Orange County or suburban Chicago. *The Book of Church Order of the Presbyterian Church of America* prudently requires that "No person should be invited to preach in any of the churches under our care without the consent of the Session." The authority that

God has established inside the church is responsible for the teaching within the church. But when you buy music written by people you do not know and use it wihout discerning, critical examination, you are inviting every error imaginable into the congregation.

I cannot stress the need for vigilance and oversight in this matter enough. Even my own denominational hymnal, which is quite good, has a hymn by a Unitarian! And once you know that, it is not hard to see that false teacher's object. Are your people in grave danger of becoming Unitarians because they sing this hymn? Probably not. But the effects of wrong singing are insidious, like Bunyan's Pilgrim being waylaid in the dungeon of Giant Despair or going down the wrong path because of the words of the Flatterer. Be vigilant.

7. *We need to trim our music consumption.* All of us understand that we could buy white sugar and consume it all day, but we know this would not be good for us. The world's use of music is like an unlimited intake of white sugar.

Calvin understood this problem well in an era that was not nearly so bedeviled as ours. Listen to what he said about music in his preface to the Psalter of 1543: "There is scarcely in the world anything which is more able to turn or bend this way and that than the morals of men, as Plato prudently considered it. And in fact, we find by experience that it has a sacred and almost incredible power to move hearts in one way or another. Therefore we ought to be even more diligent in regulating it in such a way that it shall be useful to us and in no way pernicious."

The philosopher and music theorist Theodore Adorno said, "We all know what happens to us when we absentmindedly turn on the radio, and this knowledge seems to relieve us of reflecting upon what it is. The phenomenon becomes a datum that must be accepted as unalterable, so to speak, a datum whose sheer obstinate existence proves it's right." Mindless consumption of music is nothing less than sloth; and like sloth, it injures by atrophy.

Here is a reformational rule of thumb: Listen to music with intent. Does that mean you must focus your entire attention upon the music? No. But when you do not give direct attention to the music, be sure that you use only music you have already extensively examined. Music is a medium that enters your soul immediately and effortlessly. In fact, the less you pay attention to it, the more access it has into your inner being. Do not abdicate responsibility for your musical consumption to someone else. Even the best intentioned disc jockey cannot know what you need. He does not know you.

8. *We need to sing more.* On one hand, we need to consume less music passively. On the other, we need to make more music actively. In your worship services, sing while you are collecting the offering and distributing the elements of the Lord's Supper. If you sing five hymns of four stanzas each in every service, it takes a total clock time of only about fifteen minutes.

If your parishioners hear some kind of environmental music two, ten, twenty, forty, or sixty hours a week, what is it that dwells in them richly? Do we really think our paltry eight minutes of hymns or thirty minutes of praise and worship choruses will suffice? Reclaim any time you can for congregational singing. Reduce or eliminate the announcements. Craft all the words you speak in the service so there is no fat. You don't have time to ooze or use heart-warming stories that help people connect with you as a genuine person. Proclaim the Law and the Gospel.

When all is said and done, however, there simply is no avoiding greater cost in communal clock time. For the word of Christ to dwell in you richly together, you have to deliberately spend time singing together, and this will be a matter of the will of the congregation, a passion for revival. Where your treasure is, there your heart is. If you sing doctrinally dense, aesthetic forms only a few minutes a week, you do not really desire the word of Christ to dwell in you richly. It is that simple.

What we have before us is a case of taking the long view, of running the race patiently. Almost every reformational measure we take will be costly and will have slow, almost immeasurable progress. As Americans, we don't like that. We want demonstrable results *now*. But if the Lord will grant us a reformation, it is our grandchildren who will benefit from the fruits of it. Let's love those grandchildren and be faithful now, for their benefit and, most of all, for God's glory.

# FOR FURTHER
# READING

Armstrong, John H., editor. *The Coming Evangelical Crisis: Current Challenges to the Authority of Scripture and the Gospel.* Chicago: Moody Press, 1996.

Boice, James Montgomery and Benjamin E. Sasse, editors. *Here We Stand: A Call from Confessing Evangelicals.* Grand Rapids, Mich.: Baker, 1996.

Dawn, Marva J. *Reaching Out Without Dumbing Down: A Theology of Worship for the Turn of the Century Culture.* Grand Rapids, Mich.: Eerdmans, 1995.

Johansson, Calvin M. *Discipling Music Ministry.* Peabody, Mass.: Hendrickson, 1992.

Leaver, Robin A. *Music as Preaching: Bach, Passions & Music in Worship.* Oxford: Latimer House, 1982.

Schalk, Carl F. *Luther on Music.* St. Louis: Concordia, 1982.

Stiller, Guenther. *Johann Sebastian Bach and Liturgical Life in Leipzig.* St. Louis: Concordia, 1984.

Veith, Gene Edward, Jr. *Postmodern Times: A Christian Guide to Contemporary Thought and Culture.* Wheaton, Ill.: Crossway Books, 1994.

White, James F. *Protestant Worship: Traditions in Transition.* Louisville: Westminster/John Knox Press, 1989.

Zuckerkandl, Victor. *The Sense of Music.* Princeton, N.J.: Princeton University Press, 1959.